TRUMPETER SWAN SURVEY
of the
ROCKY MOUNTAIN POPULATION

FALL 2002

TRUMPETER SWAN SURVEY
of the
ROCKY MOUNTAIN POPULATION

FALL 2002

U.S. Fish and Wildlife Service
Migratory Birds and State Programs
Mountain-Prairie Region
Lakewood, Colorado

February 24, 2003

Prepared by: _James A. Dubovsky_

James A. Dubovsky, Wildlife Biologist
Migratory Birds and State Programs

Reviewed by: _John E. Cornely_

John E. Cornely, Chief, Division of Migratory Bird Coordination
Migratory Birds and State Programs

Approved: _Paul E. Gertler_

Paul E. Gertler, Assistant Regional Director
Migratory Birds and State Programs

Richard A. Coleman

Rick Coleman, Regional Chief
National Wildlife Refuge System

Abstract.– Observers counted 371 swans (white birds and cygnets) in the U.S. Breeding Segment of the Rocky Mountain Population of trumpeter swans during fall of 2002, a decrease from 475 counted from comparable areas last year and the lowest count since 1993. The number of white birds (311) declined 23% from that of last year, while the number of cygnets (60) decreased by 15%. Declines occurred in all 3 states in which the Tri-state Area Flocks nest, and was greatest in Montana (-37%). Decreases in Idaho and Wyoming were 20% and 8%, respectively. The number of birds in restoration flocks also decreased 17% compared to the count from last year. The count for the Tri-state Area Flocks this year was a marked departure from their recent upward trend in numbers. The tri-state area continues to experience drought conditions, with Palmer Drought Index values the lowest recorded since surveys were initiated in the 1930s.

The Rocky Mountain Population (RMP) of trumpeter swans (*Cygnus buccinator*) consists of birds that nest primarily from western Canada southward to Nevada and Wyoming (Fig. 1). The population is comprised of several flocks that nest in different portions of the overall range. The RMP/Canadian Flocks consist of birds that summer primarily in southeastern Yukon Territory, southwestern Northwest Territories, northeastern British Columbia, Alberta, and western Saskatchewan. The Tri-state Area Flocks summer in areas at the juncture of the boundaries of Montana, Wyoming, and Idaho (hereafter termed the tri-state area) and nearby areas (Fig. 2). The RMP/Canadian and Tri-state Area flocks winter sympatrically primarily in the tri-state area. In addition, efforts have been made to establish several restoration flocks, such as those at Ruby Lake National Wildlife Refuge (NWR) in Nevada (i.e., Nevada flock) and those at Malheur NWR and Summer Lake Wildlife Management Area (WMA) and vicinity (i.e., Oregon flock), by translocating adult swans and cygnets from other portions of the RMP. These birds tend to winter in areas near those where they nest. This report contains information only from the Tri-state Area and restoration flocks, collectively referred to as the RMP/U.S. Breeding Segment. These terms for the various groups of swans are consistent with the RMP Trumpeter Swan Implementation Plan (Pacific Flyway Study Committee 2002).

The Fall Trumpeter Swan Survey is conducted annually in September. The survey is conducted cooperatively by several administrative entities and is intended to provide an accurate count of the number of RMP trumpeter swans that summer in the U.S. The history of the survey dates back to the 1930s, although methods and survey coverage have changed over time as the number of swans increased and new technologies became available. Survey methodology and coverage have remained fairly consistent since 1966 (D. Olson, pers. comm.). To be consistent with previous reports, only the data from 1967 to present were analyzed for this report. The data are used by managers to assess the annual status of the Tri-state Area Flocks and restoration flocks.

METHODS

The survey is conducted within a relatively short time frame to reduce the possibility of counting swans more than once due to movements of birds among areas. Aerial cruise surveys are used to

Fig. 1. Approximate ranges of trumpeter swans during summer (from Caithamer 2001).

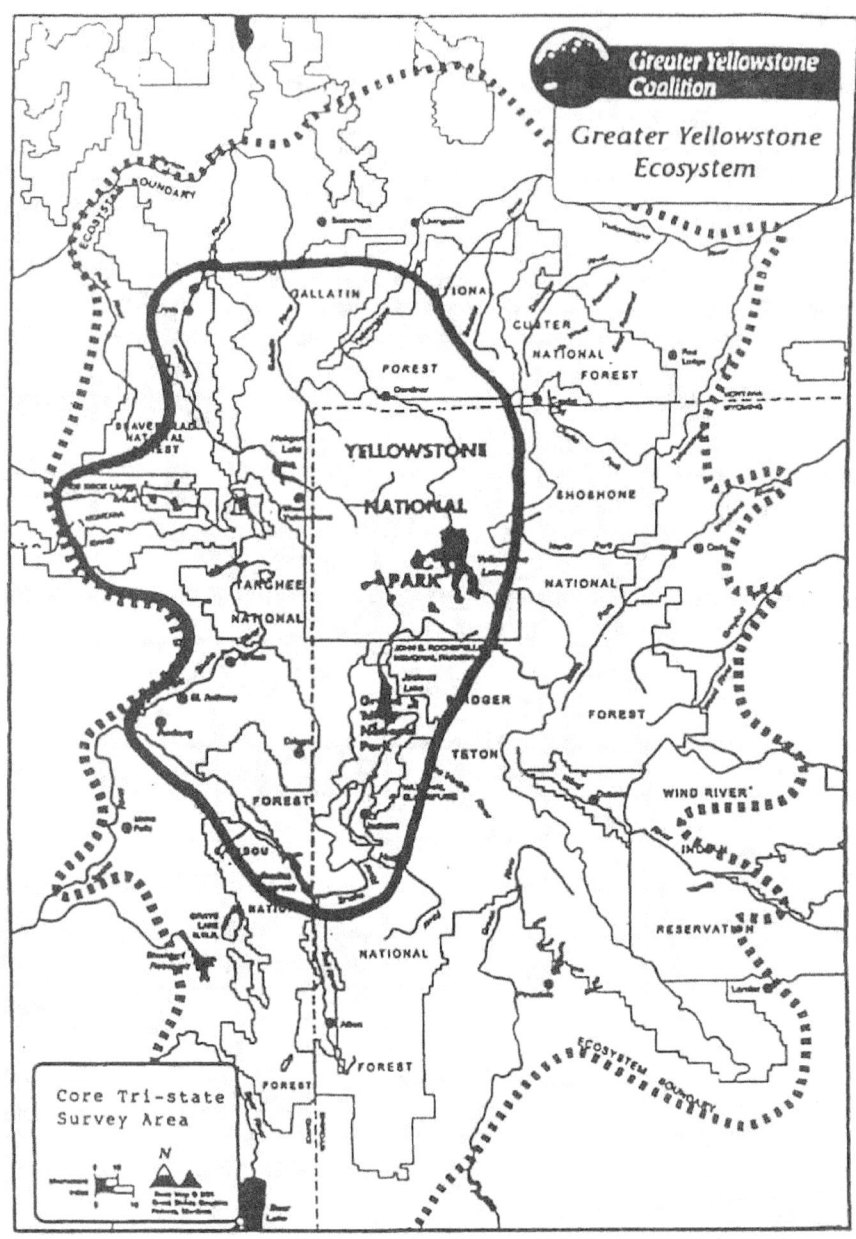

Fig. 2. Map showing the 'core' tri-state area of southeast Idaho, southwest Montana, and northwest Wyoming (provided by the Greater Yellowstone Coalition, Bozeman, Montana).

4

count numbers of swans in the tri-state area, in Nevada, and in the Summer Lake WMA and vicinity; ground surveys are used to count the number of swans at Malheur NWR and in isolated pockets of habitat not covered by aerial surveys. During aerial surveys, data are collected by observers seated in a single-engine, fixed-winged aircraft. Flying altitude varies with changes in terrain and surface winds, but generally averages 30-60 m above ground level, and flight speed is between 135-155 kph. One to two observers and the pilot count white (i.e., adults and subadults) and gray (i.e., cygnets) swans in known or suspected summer habitats. Counts are not adjusted for birds present but not seen by aerial crews, and have an unknown and unmeasured sampling variance associated with them.

During fall 2002, most of the area was surveyed during 15-19 September. Ruby Lake NWR was surveyed on 25 September. Approximately 25 h of flight time and 5 h of ground survey time were required to complete the survey. Weather conditions during this time generally were warm and sunny. However, the weather in Idaho was overcast with some showers. Many areas near the Summer Lake WMA where most swans of the Oregon flock are counted were not surveyed this fall. These were the only areas traditionally surveyed that were not completed. Oregon will attempt to conduct these surveys in the future, but resource constraints may preclude them from doing so in some years (B. Bales and M. St. Louis, Oregon Dept. of Fish and Wildlife, pers. comm.).

RESULTS AND DISCUSSION

Habitats continued to be quite dry during fall, and the tri-state area remained in a drought. By mid-June, much of the summering range of RMP swans in the U.S. was in severe to extreme drought (Fig. 3). The drought intensified further as summer progressed. Recently, Palmer Drought Indices for southwest Montana have reached their lowest levels in almost 70 years (Fig. 4). Survey biologists reported that many wetland areas were dry in September (Appendix A).

Historical Trends

During 1988-92, several significant management actions affecting the RMP/U.S. Breeding Segment occurred concurrently, including (1) the hazing of swans from wintering areas to alleviate high concentrations of birds, (2) experimental translocations of many swans from summer and winter areas to alternate sites to promote use of new wintering areas and establish alternative migratory pathways (Shea and Drewien 1999), and (3) the termination of winter feeding of swans at Red Rock Lakes NWR (U.S. Fish and Wildlife Service 1992). Collectively, these actions likely influenced the demographics of these birds, and the number of swans declined markedly (-46%) between the falls of 1988 and 1993. Because the management actions mentioned above likely impacted swans in the RMP/U.S. Breeding Segment and the Tri-state Area Flocks, we partitioned the data from 1967-2001 into two time periods to assess trends in swan abundance prior to 1989 and after 1992. The first period encompassed the fall counts from 1967-88, years during which swans were provided winter food at Red Rock Lakes NWR, and translocations of cygnets and adults during fall occurred (Gale et al. 1988) but at a relatively low level (averages of about 2 cygnets and 3 adults per year) compared to 1988-92 when about 11 juveniles and 29 adults per year were translocated during summer (data

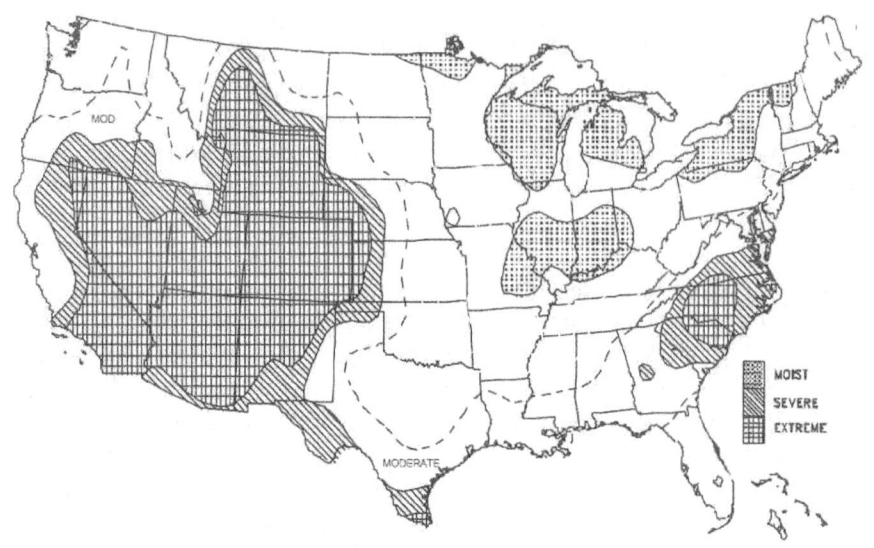

Fig. 3. Palmer Drought Index map for June 22, 2002 (Joint Agricultural Weather Facility 2002).

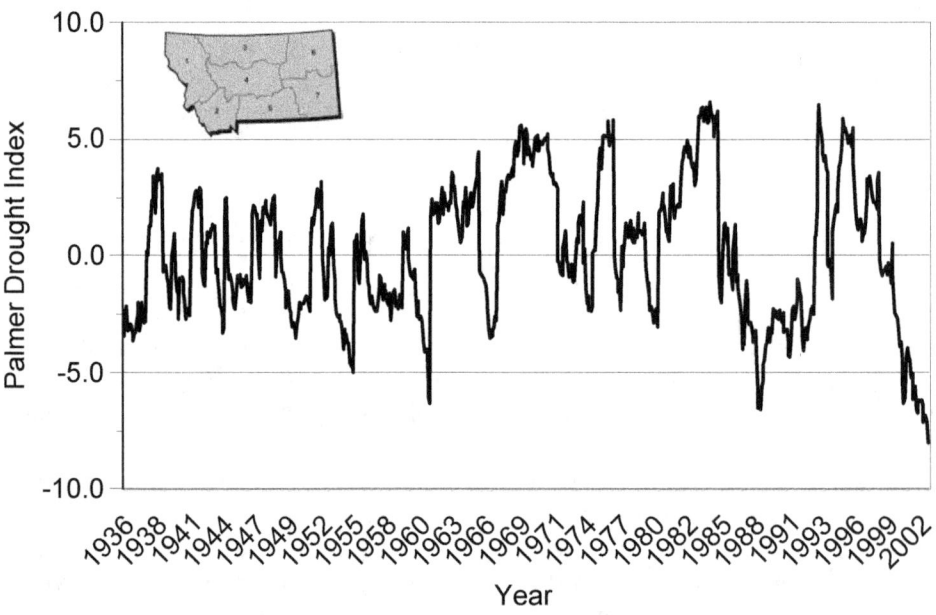

Fig. 4. Monthly Palmer Drought Indices for climate division 2 in southwest Montana.

in Shea and Drewien 1999). The second time period analyzed included counts from 1993-2001, immediately following the termination of winter feeding and the summer-translocation experiment. Counts for the Oregon flock also were divided into 2 time periods for analysis, but the periods were different from those used for analysis of the RMP/U.S. Breeding Segment and the Tri-state Area Flocks. Between the winters of 1991-1995, almost 600 birds wintering in Harriman State Park, Idaho and over 50 birds summering at Red Rock Lakes NWR were translocated to the Summer Lake WMA (Shea and Drewien 1999). Because of this large influx of birds, we analyzed the counts for the period prior to the translocations (i.e., 1967-91) separate from counts that occurred once the translocations were initiated (i.e., 1992-2001). Counts for the Nevada flock probably were not influenced to a large extent by any of the management actions mentioned above for the Tri-state Area and Oregon flocks (i.e., the Nevada flock is spatially disjunct from the other flocks, and no swans were moved to Nevada during 1988-96 [Shea and Drewien 1999]). Therefore, we did not partition the data for the Nevada flock, and used the entire time series of counts in analyses.

We used least-squares regression on log-transformed counts to assess changes in growth rates within the time periods analyzed for each of the swan flocks. Counts from the current fall survey (2002) were compared to results from the earlier time frames, a practice used in U.S. Fish and Wildlife Service survey reports for other waterfowl (e.g., Wilkins and Otto 2002, U.S. Fish and Wildlife Service 2002).

The counts for total swans of the RMP/U.S. Breeding Segment suggested no trend ($P = 0.27$) during 1967-88 (Table 1, Fig. 5). The number of white birds appeared to decline slightly (-0.8% per year), but the value for the slope parameter (β) was only marginally significant (P [$\beta<0$] = 0.16). The counts for cygnets suggested no trend ($P = 0.50$). During 1993-2001, counts of total swans (+2.4% per year) and counts of white birds (+ 2.9% per year) increased (P [$\beta>0$] ≤ 0.10), but no trend in the number of cygnets was evident ($P = 0.76$). Patterns for regression statistics for the Tri-state Area Flocks were similar to those for the RMP/U.S. Breeding Segment (Fig. 6), because the vast majority of birds comprising the RMP/U.S. Breeding Segment summer in the tri-state area (Table 1). However, the counts of white swans appeared to decline at a somewhat greater rate (-1.0% per year, $P = 0.09$) during 1967-88, and counts of total and white swans increased (+3.6% and +4.0% per year, respectively)($P \leq 0.02$) at greater rates during 1993-2001 compared to the entire RMP/U.S. Breeding Segment.

Birds summering in Montana (Table 2) had patterns of change relatively similar to that of the Tri-state Area Flocks as a whole, because historically the swans in Montana comprised the majority of birds in the Tri-state Area Flocks. Total swans in Montana appeared to decline slightly (-1.2% per year) during 1967-88 (Fig. 7), although the value for the slope parameter was only marginally significant ($P = 0.16$). The decline existed only for white birds; counts for cygnets suggested no trend ($P = 0.95$). However, swans in Montana increased from 1993-2001 at a greater rate ($\beta = +6.9\%$ per year, $P < 0.01$) than that for the Tri-state Area Flocks as a whole, resulting from increases in the number of white birds. In Idaho, no trends in total or white swan counts were evident for the 1967-88 period, but the counts for cygnets increased ($P = 0.03$) (Fig. 8). During 1993-2001, a 2.8% per year increase in the number of total swans was marginally significant ($P = 0.16$). No trends in

7

Table 1. Counts of trumpeter swans of the Rocky Mountain Population during fall, 1967-2002.

Year	Tri-state Area Flocks			Restoration flocks			RMP/U.S. Breeding Segment		
	White birds	Cygnets	Total	White birds	Cygnets	Total	White birds	Cygnets	Total
1967	520	45	565	60	13	73	580	58	638
1968	431	154	585	58	20	78	489	174	663
1969	a			69	23	92			
1970				45	16	61			
1971	431	68	499	46	27	73	477	95	572
1972				42	16	58			
1973				42	7	49			
1974	457	80	537	35	9	44	492	89	581
1975				41	9	50			
1976				31	9	40			
1977	403	86	489	51	4	55	454	90	544
1978				39	15	54			
1979				41	42	83			
1980	462	23	485	71	26	97	533	49	582
1981				77	14	91			
1982				56	20	76			
1983	398	54	452	73	22	95	471	76	547
1984	431	58	489	65	9	74	496	67	563
1985	368	139	507	63	5	68	431	144	575
1986	331	61	392	34	26	60	365	87	452
1987	365	175	540	52	19	71	417	194	611
1988	464	137	601	49	9	58	513	146	659
1989	505	60	565	30	3	33	535	63	598
1990	432	147	579	36	11	47	468	158	626
1991	414	91	505	32	18	50	446	109	555
1992	390	92	482	75	6	81	465	98	563
1993	248	29	277	55	22	77	303	51	354
1994	239	130	369	63	22	85	302	152	454
1995	307	55	362	58	7	65	365	62	427
1996	316	63	379	64	15	79	380	78	458
1997	310	54	364	48	15	63	358	69	427
1998	304	90	394	60	15	75	364	105	469
1999	312	56	368	35	14	49	347	70	417
2000	324	102	426	48	7	55	372	109	481
2001	362	59	421	54	12	66	416	71	487
2002	273	53	326	38b	7b	45b	311b	60b	371b

[a] Blank denotes value not calculated because of incomplete survey.

[b] Data for only Malheur NWR and the Nevada flock included; Summer Lake WMA survey not completed.

8

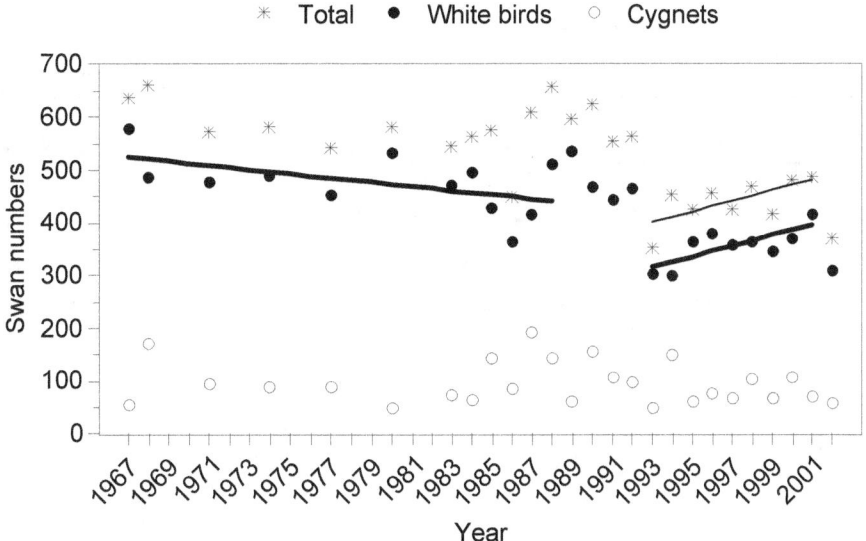

Fig. 5. Counts of swans in the RMP/U.S. Breeding Segment during the Fall Trumpeter Swan Survey, 1967-2002 (thin and thick lines depict trends for total swans and white birds, respectively). The count for 2002 is from an incomplete survey, and is not directly comparable to prior years.

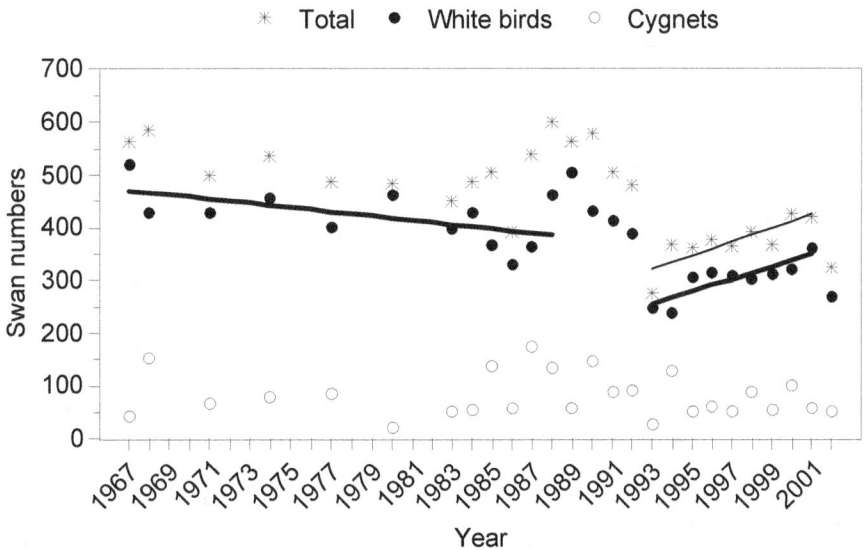

Fig. 6. Counts of swans in the Tri-state Area Flocks during the Fall Trumpeter Swan Survey, 1967-2002 (thin and thick lines depict trends for total swans and white birds, respectively).

9

Table 2. Counts of trumpeter swans of the Rocky Mountain Population U.S. Breeding Segment in individual states during fall, 1967-2002.

Year	Montana White birds	Montana Cygnets	Montana Total	Idaho White birds	Idaho Cygnets	Idaho Total	Wyoming White birds	Wyoming Cygnets	Wyoming Total	Oregon White birds	Oregon Cygnets	Oregon Total	Nevada White birds	Nevada Cygnets	Nevada Total
1967	334	25	359	87	8	95	99	12	111	33	12	45	27	1	28
1968	242	123	365	88	6	94	101	25	126	34	11	45	24	9	33
1969	a									36	14	50	33	9	42
1970										37	13	50	8	3	11
1971	297	49	346	60	6	66	74	13	87	38	22	60	8	5	13
1972										32	13	45	10	3	13
1973										36	4	40	6	3	9
1974	296	49	345	71	17	88	90	14	104	29	9	38	6	0	6
1975										33	7	40	8	2	10
1976										23	8	31	8	1	9
1977	267	64	331	60	7	67	76	15	91	33	0	33	18	4	22
1978										24	13	37	15	2	17
1979	324	63	387							31	33	64	10	9	19
1980	315	6	321	73	11	84	74	6	80	53	15	68	18	11	29
1981										53	9	62	24	5	29
1982										38	17	55	18	3	21
1983	228	32	260	92	6	98	78	16	94	55	17	72	18	5	23
1984	268	22	290	80	21	101	83	15	98	40	6	46	25	3	28
1985	212	87	299	83	27	110	73	25	98	38	2	40	25	3	28
1986	174	28	202	83	14	97	74	19	93	19	24	43	15	2	17
1987	210	133	343	63	15	78	92	27	119	38	14	52	14	5	19
1988	268	77	345	87	28	115	109	32	141	33	8	41	16	1	17
1989	294	23	317	101	16	117	110	21	131	20	3	23	10	0	10
1990	245	108	353	92	28	120	95	11	106	27	7	34	9	4	13
1991	176	60	236	138	26	164	100	5	105	24	14	38	8	4	12
1992	156	74	230	109	8	117	125	10	135	62	6	68	13	0	13
1993	60	16	76	94	6	100	94	7	101	47	17	64	8	5	13
1994	70	48	118	79	49	128	90	33	123	48	13	61	15	9	24
1995	84	17	101	118	21	139	105	17	122	45	6	51	13	1	14
1996	95	36	131	127	20	147	94	7	101	49	10	59	15	5	20
1997	88	18	106	112	19	131	110	17	127	31	9	40	17	6	23
1998	105	35	140	110	37	147	89	18	107	39	8	47	21	7	28
1999	120	21	141	103	23	126	89	12	101	19	9	28	16	5	21
2000	127	24	151	102	40	142	95	38	133	22	5	27	26	2	28
2001	140	9	149	124	23	147	98	27	125	23	12	35	31	0	31
2002	76	18	94	103	14	117	94	21	115	14b	7b	21b	24	0	24

[a] Blank denotes survey was not conducted.

[b] Counts for Malheur NWR only; Summer Lake WMA survey not completed.

swan counts were evident in Wyoming (Fig. 9). However, counts during the 1993-2001 period generally were as high or higher than counts during the 1967-88 period.

No trend was evident in counts of total swans or white birds for the Oregon flock during the period 1967-91 ($P \geq 0.34$) (Fig. 10). However, during 1992-2001, total swans decreased 10.0% per year ($P < 0.01$), and the rate of decrease in the number of white birds was 12.0% per year ($P < 0.01$). The counts of cygnets suggested no trend over the entire time frame ($P = 0.22$). Apparently, the large number of birds moved to Summer Lake WMA either did not survive or moved elsewhere over time. Further, the number of total swans during the last few years is somewhat lower than that during the 1960s. Recent declines at Malheur NWR may partly be the result of moving birds from Malheur NWR to nearby Summer Lake WMA during the 1990s (M. Laws, Malheur NWR, pers. comm.); modeling exercises suggest source areas may be depleted as a result of removals (Page 1976, but see Turner 1981).

Counts for the Nevada flock ranged between 6 and 42 birds during 1967-2001, with no apparent long-term trends in either white birds or cygnets (Fig. 11). However, counts of white birds in recent years have been near historic highs, and the total counts generally have increased over the short-term (i.e., last 10 years).

Results from the 2002 survey

Because areas near the Summer Lake WMA were not surveyed this year, the fall 2001 survey data were recalculated excluding the Summer Lake WMA data to permit meaningful comparisons between 2002 and 2001 counts of the RMP/U.S. Breeding Segment. During fall 2002, observers counted 371 trumpeter swans for the RMP/U.S. Breeding Segment, a decrease of 22% from the count (475) for comparable areas last year and the lowest count since 1993 (Fig. 5). Both the number of white birds (-23%) and cygnets (-15%) declined from their respective counts last year. These drops are in contrast to the upward trend in swan abundance observed during 1993-2001.

Decreases were noted throughout the surveyed area. The largest decline in total swans from 2001 counts occurred in Montana (-37%), followed by Idaho (-20%), restoration flocks (-17%), and Wyoming (-8%). The number of white birds declined in all areas surveyed (Table 2), but was especially pronounced in Montana (-46%). The number of swans at Malheur NWR in 2002 was only slightly above record lows. In Nevada, the number of white birds declined from the second-highest count last year, but remains high relative to the long-term (i.e., 1967-2001) average. For the first time since 1996, movement by white birds into Yellowstone National Park appears to have occurred (5 total; 2 into northern and 3 into southern areas [T. McEneaney, pers. comm.]); however, the significance of these observations is undetermined.

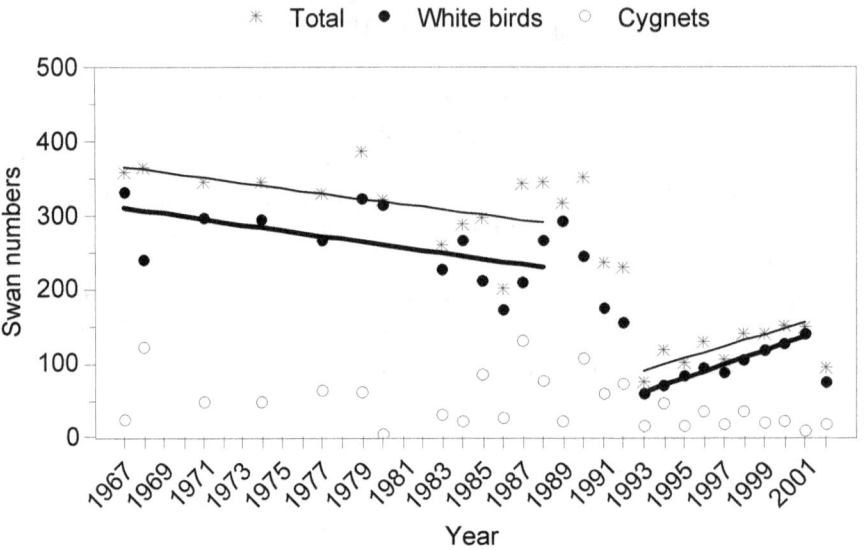

Fig. 7. Numbers of swans counted in Montana during the Fall Trumpeter Swan Survey, 1967-2002 (thin and thick lines depict trends for total swans and white birds, respectively).

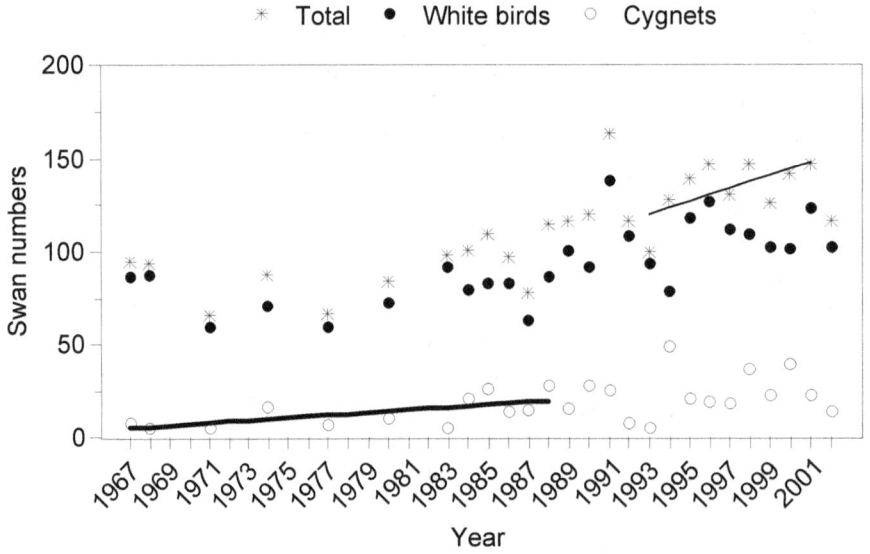

Fig. 8. Numbers of swans counted in Idaho during the Fall Trumpeter Swan Survey, 1967-2002 (thin and thick lines depict trends for total swans and cygnets, respectively).

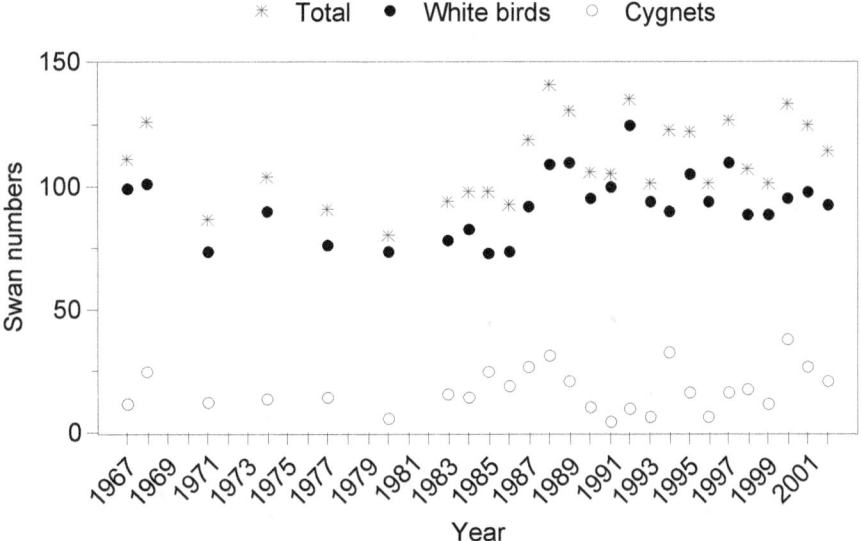

Fig. 9. Numbers of swans counted in Wyoming during the Fall Trumpeter Swan Survey, 1967-2002.

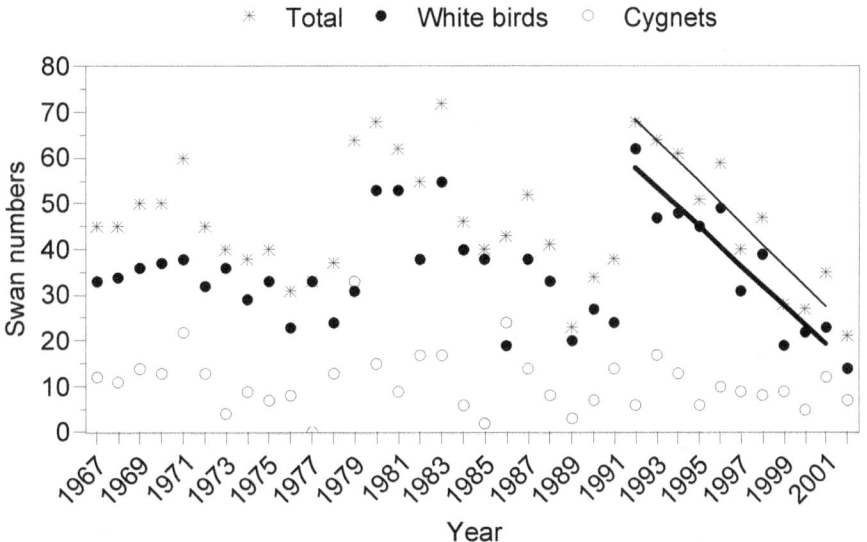

Fig. 10. Numbers of swans counted in the Oregon flock during the Fall Trumpeter Swan Survey, 1967-2002 (thin and thick lines depict trends for total swans and white birds, respectively). The count for 2002 is from an incomplete survey, and is not comparable to prior years.

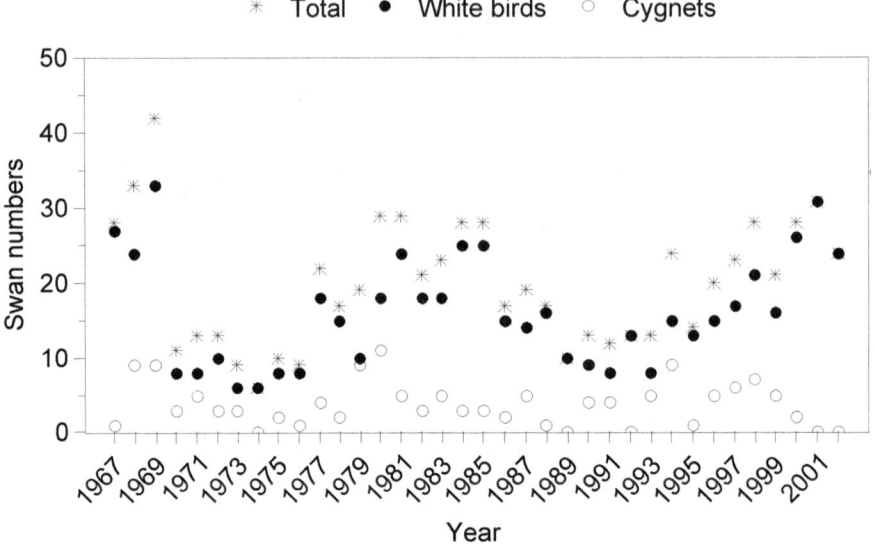

Fig. 11. Numbers of swans counted in the Nevada flock during the Fall Trumpeter Swan Survey, 1967-2002.

The production of cygnets increased in Montana, but declined in other areas. An index[1] to production rate (i.e., cygnets/white birds) in Montana (0.237) was near the long-term (i.e., 1967-2001) average (0.267), but rates in Wyoming (0.226) and at Malheur NWR (0.500) were somewhat higher than their respective averages (0.193 and 0.390). The rate in Idaho (0.136) was substantially below average (0.208). For the second consecutive year, the Nevada flock fledged no cygnets.

Changes in point counts of animals can be influenced by several factors (i.e., mortality, animal movements, survey problems). The lower count of swans in the Tri-state Area Flocks observed in 2002 could be the result of one or more of these phenomena. Given the information available, we cannot ascertain which cause or causes for the decline are most likely. To date, we have no evidence to suggest that a large amount of mortality occurred. Weather in the tri-state area during winter 2001-02 was relatively mild, and biologists believe mild weather may enhance winter survival of swans in this region. Observers traversing the tri-state area to detect neck-collared swans documented the mortality of a similar number of swans to that of the previous winter (i.e., 32 during winter 2000-01, 34 during winter 2001-02 [Whitman 2002]). We do not know what proportion of the dead birds were from nesting areas in Canada versus those nesting in the U.S., so we cannot directly attribute this level of winter mortality to numerical changes in the Tri-state Area Flocks. Winter counts of RMP swans in the tri-state area were 3,917 and 4,360 during winters 2001 and 2002, respectively (Olson 2001, 2002). Of the 7 swans with neck collars that died during winters 2000-02 (S. Bouffard, Minidoka NWR, pers. comm.), 3 of the birds had been sighted in Canada at least once, and 3 birds died the same winter in which they were banded so their breeding-ground affinity could not be surmised. The remaining swan was resighted only in Idaho during each of 6 winters. However, all of the sightings of this bird were between 8 November and 25 March, so the breeding-ground affinity of this bird also is uncertain. Finally, observations by biologists through April also did not document significant incidences of mortality in late spring (D. Munoz, Southeast Idaho Refuge Complex, pers. comm.).

Nonetheless, no systematic surveys to detect swan mortality are conducted. In many instances, dead swans are detected by casual observations of individuals. Therefore, our ability to detect changes in mortality is limited, especially if that mortality is at a relatively low level over a broad expanse of land or if it occurs in areas that are not typically visited.

The count this fall departed substantially from the upward trend in swan numbers since 1992, and monitoring data currently available do not allow us to determine a biological cause for the sudden and dramatic decline. Certainly, the count should be cause for concern. However, at this point data

---

[1] A better method to assess annual productivity is to estimate the number of young produced per breeding pair, because a proportion of white birds each year are subabults or adults that did not nest. Traditionally, such information was provided in this report. However, those data are not collected as part of the Fall Trumpeter Swan Survey. In past reports, methods describing how the data are collected, areas covered, and effort expended have not been reported. Further, issues regarding proprietary rights to those data have been raised. For these reasons the data have not been included in this report. Recently, the Greater Yellowstone Trumpeter Swan Working Group (GYTSWG) has been tasked with developing data-collection protocols and reporting formats (Pacific Flyway Study Committee 2002:14). The issue of how those data are reported should be discussed by the GYTSWG.

do not exist that indicate the decrease is due entirely to mortality, or to confirm that the size of the Tri-state Area Flocks has been reduced by 23%. Nonetheless, we also should not simply dismiss the number as an aberration. Survey results for the next few years will be critical to assess whether the decrease in birds counted this year is an anomaly or an indication of changing demographics.

ACKNOWLEDGMENTS

We would like to especially thank the personnel who conducted the surveys, a list of whom is provided in Appendix B. The survey is a collaborative effort among Red Rock Lakes NWR, Migratory Birds and State Programs -- Mountain-Prairie Region of the U.S. Fish and Wildlife Service, Southeast Idaho Refuge Complex, National Elk Refuge, Harriman State Park, Idaho Department of Fish and Game, Grand Teton National Park, Yellowstone National Park, Wyoming Game and Fish Department, Ruby Lake NWR, Malheur NWR, and the Shoshone-Bannock Tribes. S. Comeau compiled the data. S. Bouffard (Minidoka NWR) provided resighting data for neck-collared swans. S. Comeau, J. Cornely, M. Laws, T. McEneaney, C. Mitchell, S. Patla, J. Mackay, and D. Olson reviewed a previous draft of this document. S. Bouffard and R. Shea also provided comments.

LITERATURE CITED

Caithamer, D.F. 2001. Trumpeter swan population status, 2000. U.S. Fish and Wildlife Service, Division of Migratory Bird Management, Laurel, MD. 14pp.

Gale, R.S., E.O. Garton, and I.J. Ball. 1988. The history, ecology and management of the Rocky Mountain Population of trumpeter swans. Unpublished report. U.S. Fish and Wildlife Service, Montana Cooperative Wildlife Research Unit, Missoula. 532pp.

Joint Agricultural Weather Facility. 1992. Weekly Weather and Crop Bulletin. Vol. 89, No. 26. URL:http://usda.mannlib.cornell.edu/reports/waobr/weather/2002/full/wwcb2602.pdf.

Olson, D. 2001. 2001 mid-winter trumpeter swan survey. U.S. Fish and Wildlife Service, Red Rock Lakes National Wildlife Refuge, Lakeview, MT. 10pp. plus tables and figures.

Olson, D. 2002. 2002 mid-winter trumpeter swan survey. U.S. Fish and Wildlife Service, Red Rock Lakes National Wildlife Refuge, Lakeview, MT. 8pp. plus tables and figures.

Pacific Flyway Study Committee. 2002. RMP Trumpeter Swan Implementation Plan. U.S. Fish and Wildlife Service, Portland, OR. 27pp.

Page, R.D. 1976. The ecology of the trumpeter swan on Red Rock Lakes National Wildlife Refuge. Ph.D. dissertation. University of Montana, Missoula. 160pp.

Shea, R.E., and R.C. Drewien. 1999. Evaluation of efforts to redistribute the Rocky Mountain Population of trumpeter swans, 1986-97. Unpublished report. 51pp. plus table and figures.

Turner, B.C. 1981. Status of the Grande Prairie trumpeter swan population and its habitat. Unpublished report. Canadian Wildlife Service, Edmonton, Alberta. 13pp.

U.S. Fish and Wildlife Service. 1992. Environmental Assessment for proposed termination of winter feeding of trumpeter swans at Red Rock Lakes National Wildlife Refuge. U.S. Fish and Wildlife Service, Red Rock Lakes National Wildlife Refuge, Lakeview, MT. 26pp.

U.S. Fish and Wildlife Service. 2002. Waterfowl population status, 2002. U.S. Department of the Interior, Washington, D.C. 51pp.

Whitman, C. 2002. Causes of trumpeter swan mortalities observed in southwestern Montana, eastern Idaho, and northwestern Wyoming during the winters of 2000 and 2001. Unpublished report. U.S. Fish and Wildlife Service, Southeast Idaho Refuge Complex, Pocatello. 8pp. plus tables.

Wilkins, K.A., and M.C. Otto. 2002. Trends in duck breeding populations, 1955-2002. U.S. Fish and Wildlife Service Administrative Report, Division of Migratory Bird Management, Laurel, MD. 19pp.

Appendix A. Site-specific counts of trumpeter swans of the Rocky Mountain Population-U.S. Breeding Segment during the Fall Trumpeter Swan Survey, 2002.

Montana	White birds	Cygnets	Total	Pilot/observer/notes
Red Rock Lakes NWR				O: S. Comeau, G. Dehmer; P: B. Twist (9/19)
Upper Red Rock Lake	21	0	21	
Upper Lake Outlet to River Marsh	4	0	4	
Swan Lake	1	0	1	
Shambo Pond	0	0	0	
Lower Red Rock Lake	0	0	0	
West Pintail Ditch	0	0	0	
Widgeon Pond	0	0	0	
Sparrow Slough	0	0	0	Dry
Sparrow Pond	0	0	0	Dry
Culver Pond	0	0	0	
MacDonald Pond	2	5	7	
ElkSprings Creek	0	0	0	
Tucks Slough	0	0	0	Dry
Red Rock Creek	13	0	13	
Antelope Pond	0	0	0	
Sora Pond	0	0	0	
Subtotal	**41**	**5**	**46**	
Centennial Valley (CV)				
Red Rock River	19	7	26	
Lima Reservoir	0	0	0	Nearly dry
Blake Slough	0	0	0	
Twin Forks wetland	0	0	0	
Conklin Lake	2	2	4	
Elk Lake	0	0	0	
7L Wetland	0	0	0	Dry
Mud Lake	0	0	0	Dry
Stibal Pond	0	0	0	Dry
Huntsman Pond	0	0	0	
Scheid Stock Pond	0	0	0	
Jones Pond	0	0	0	Dry
Winslow Pond	0	0	0	
Winslow Creek	0	0	0	
Bean Creek Pond (tooth pond)	2	0	2	
Subtotal	**23**	**9**	**32**	
Madison Valley				
Ennis Lake	1	0	1	
Walsh Ponds	0	0	0	
Madison River	0	0	0	
Hidden Lake	0	0	0	
Otter & Goose Lake	0	0	0	

18

Cliff Lake	0	0	0	
Wade Lake	0	0	0	
Tributary to Odell Creek	0	0	0	
Quake Lake	0	0	0	
Hebgen Lake	0	0	0	
Subtotal	**1**	**0**	**1**	
Paradise Valley				O: T. McEneaney; P: R. Stradley (9/19)
Call of the Wild Ranch - DePuy's	2	0	2	
Call of the Wild Ranch - Lower DePuy's	1	1	2	
Call of the Wild Range - Upper DePuy's	2	0	2	
Baileys	2	0	2	
Brandis' Diamond B Ranch	4	3	7	
Dana's	0	0	0	
Emigrant Pond	0	0	0	
Subtotal	**11**	**4**	**15**	
Idaho				
Island Park/Upper Henry's Fork				O: C. Mitchell; P: G. Lust (9/17-18)
Henry's Lake	0	0	0	
Henry's Lake Flat	0	0	0	
North Fork area/Mack's Inn	0	0	0	Big Springs to Mack's Inn
Henry's Fork	0	0	0	Mack's Inn to Island Park Reservoir
Subtotal	**0**	**0**	**0**	
Shotgun Valley				
South Shore Island Park Reservoir	0	0	0	Reservoir very low
Sheep Creek Reservoir	0	0	0	
Icehouse Reservoir	13	0	13	1 green collar observed
Shotgun Reservoir	0	0	0	
North shoreline Island Park Reservoir	0	0	0	
Sheridan Reservoir	4	0	4	
Sheridan Creek (cabin with pond)	0	0	0	
Subtotal	**17**	**0**	**17**	
Harriman State Park				
Henry's Fork above Osbourne Bridge	6	0	6	
Henry's Fork below Osbourne Bridge	5	0	5	
Silver Lake	2	0	2	
Golden Lake	2	0	2	
Pond east-northeast of Golden Lake	0	0	0	
Thurman Creek	0	0	0	
Fish Pond	0	0	0	
Subtotal	**15**	**0**	**15**	

Appendix A. (cont.)

Upper Henry's Fork Area				
Buffalo River	0	0	0	
H. Fork-Box Canyon to Harriman State Park	0	0	0	Island Park Dam to Harriman State Park
Trude Siding-Pond/Elk Creek complex	1	0	1	
Pond on Split Creek	a			Not surveyed; poor habitat
Tom's Creek	0	0	0	
Blue Spring	0	0	0	
Last Chance Pond-north	0	0	0	
Last Chance Pond-south	0	0	0	
Henry's Fork below Pine Haven	0	0	0	
Boy Scout (Boundary) Pond	0	0	0	Should be called 'Boy Scout Rec. Pond'
Unnamed wetland #3	0	0	0	Should be called 'Boy Scout/boundary Pond'
Eccles East	0	0	0	cattle pond -- can delete
Unnamed wetland #2	0	0	0	Dry
Unnamed wetland #4	0	0	0	Should be called 'State Section Pond'
Unnamed wetland #2	0	0	0	Renamed wetland #5; dry
Unnamed wetland #1	0	0	0	Should be called 'Eccles West'; dry
Swan Lake (west)	0	0	0	Mostly dry
Hatchery Butte Road ponds	0	0	0	
Lilypad Lake (Pineview)	0	0	0	Should be called 'Lily Pond'; mostly dry
Hatchery Butte	0	0	0	Dry
North of Hatchery Butte	0	0	0	Water very low
Beaver Pond (Gerrit)	0	0	0	
Railroad Pond	2	0	2	
Pond northeast of Gerrit	0	0	0	
Mesa Marsh	2	0	2	
Northwest of Mesa Marsh	0	0	0	
Bear Lake	1	0	1	Bear and Cub Lakes
Twin Lakes	2	0	2	
Porcupine Lake	0	0	0	
Beaver Lake	0	0	0	Dry
Rock Creek	0	0	0	
Lower Goose Lake	0	0	0	
Upper Goose Lake	2	0	2	
Long Meadows	0	0	0	
Swan Lake (east-Falls River)	0	0	0	
Steele Lake	0	0	0	
Putney Meadows	0	0	0	Mostly dry
Falls River Ridge Ponds	0	0	0	
Thompson's Hole	0	0	0	
Pond west of Thompson's Hole	2	0	2	
Chain Lakes	2	0	2	
Fall River Canyon	0	0	0	
Horseshoe Lake	0	0	0	
Tule Lake	0	0	0	
McReynolds Reservoir	0	0	0	
Subtotal	**14**	**0**	**14**	

Appendix A. (cont.)

Lower Henry's Fork				
Upper Arcadia Reservoir	0	0	0	
Lower Arcadia Reservoir	2	0	2	
Marsh northwest of Upper Arcadia Reservoir	2	0	2	
Mikesell Reservoir 1	0	0	0	
Mikesell Reservoir 2	0	0	0	
Sand Creek Wildlife Management Area	3	0	3	
Wetlands west of Ashton	0	0	0	
Willow Creek ponds	0	0	0	
Chester Reservoir	0	0	0	
West of Chester Dam	1	0	1	
Singleton Ponds	1	0	1	
Lemon Lake	0	0	0	
Mackerts Pond	0	0	0	
Pond +/- 1 mile north of St. Anthony	0	0	0	
Ponds west of Menan Buttes	0	0	0	
Lower Henry's Fork to east of Market Lake	2	0	2	
Subtotal	**11**	**0**	**11**	
Camas NWR				
Toomey Pond	0	0	0	
2-Way Pond	2	3	5	
Rays Lake	0	0	0	
Center Pond	0	0	0	
Big Pond	2	0	2	
First pond north of Sandhole Lake	2	0	2	Pond west of Sandhole Lake
Mud Lake Wildlife Management Area	0	0	0	
Market Lake Wildlife Management Area	0	0	0	Mostly dry
Teton Basin	0	0	0	
Subtotal	**6**	**3**	**9**	
Grays Lake NWR				
Shorty's Cabin	0	0	0	Mostly dry
Buck Lake (west of Bear Island)	0	0	0	Mostly dry
Big Springs Area	2	0	2	Mostly dry
Bishop Island	0	0	0	Mostly dry
B Riley Point (northwest of Bear Island)	0	0	0	Mostly dry
Outlet (main)	5	0	5	
Big Bend Marsh	4	0	4	
Brockman Creek	5	4	9	Off refuge
Outlet Creek (north of road)	0	0	0	
North Canal	0	0	0	
South Canal	0	0	0	
Lakefront ponds (west of Headquarters)	0	0	0	Mostly dry
Kackley/Gravel Creek	0	0	0	

Appendix A. (cont.)

Beavertail	2	0	2	Mostly dry
Crane Reservoir (Little Valley)	0	0	0	Off refuge
Chubb Springs	0	0	0	Off refuge
Subtotal	**18**	**4**	**22**	
Soda Springs Area				
5-Mile Meadow	0	0	0	
Miller Pond	0	0	0	
Soda Creek - Miller > Cellan Reservoir	0	0	0	
Cellan Reservoir	8	0	8	
Soda Creek-spring creek west of Soda Springs	0	0	0	Pond north of here has 2 mute swans
Chester Basin	0	0	0	
Alexander Reservoir	0	0	0	
Alexander Siding	0	0	0	
Woodall Ponds	0	0	0	
Subtotal	**8**	**0**	**8**	
Bear Lake NWR				
Rainbow Unit	2	4	6	
Alder Unit	0	0	0	
MudLake Unit	2	0	2	
Salt Meadow Unit	0	0	0	
Dingle Unit	0	0	0	
West Canal Unit	0	0	0	
Bloomington Unit	2	0	2	
Subtotal	**6**	**4**	**10**	
Fort Hall Bottoms				
Head of Clear Creek	0	0	0	Clear Creek above Sheepskin Road
American Falls Reservoir-northwest corner	5	0	5	
Kinney Creek	0	0	0	
Clear Creek - middle	0	0	0	Clear Creek below Sheepskin Road
Mouth of Portneuf River	0	0	0	
Flying Y	0	0	0	
Diggie Creek & sloughs on Broncho Road	0	0	0	
Springfield Reservoir	0	0	0	
Sterling Wildlife Management Area	0	0	0	
Subtotal	**5**	**0**	**5**	
Other Idaho				
Chesterfield	0	0	0	Dry
Chicken Creek wetland	0	0	0	
Wetlands east of Blackfoot	0	0	0	
Subtotal	**0**	**0**	**0**	

Appendix A. (cont.)

Lower Snake River				
American Falls Reservoir - Minidoka NWR	0	0	0	
C. J. Strike Reservoir	0	0	0	
Subtotal	**0**	**0**	**0**	
Minidoka NWR	**0**	**0**	**0**	
Central & Western Idaho				
White Arrow Ponds (Bliss)	0	0	0	
Fairfield Gravel Pit	3	3	6	Idaho Fish and Game ground survey
Silver Creek (Picabo)				
Oxford Slough Waterfowl Production Area	0	0	0	Dry
Swan Lake (Bannock County)	0	0	0	Mostly dry
Subtotal	**3**	**3**	**6**	
Wyoming				
Yellowstone National Park				O: T. McEneaney; P: R. Stradley (9/19)
Geode Pond	0	0	0	
Crescent Pond	0	0	0	
Slough Creek	2	0	2	
Tern Lake	0	0	0	
Yellowstone Lake, southeast arm west of Molly Islands	2	0	2	
Yellowstone Lake, southeast arm - Yellowstone Delta	2	0	2	
Beach Springs	0	0	0	
Heart Lake	0	0	0	
Yellowstone River, Alum-Grizzly Overlook	1	0	1	
Yellowstone River, north of Fishing Bridge	2	0	2	
Boundary Creek	3	0	3	
Boundary Creek Pond	2	0	2	
Buela Meadow (Lake)	0	0	0	
Lillypad Lake	0	0	0	
Junco Lake	0	0	0	
Riddle Lake	2	4	6	
Robinson Lake	0	0	0	
West Robinson Lake	0	0	0	
Bechler River	1	0	1	
Lower Madison River	1	0	1	Seven-mile bridge
Nymph Lake	0	0	0	
Grizzly Lake	2	0	2	
Obsidian Lake	0	0	0	
Trumpeter Lake	0	0	0	
North Kidney Lake	0	0	0	
Grebe Lake	0	0	0	
South Arm - Grouse	0	0	0	

East end of Mary Bay	0	0	0	
Delusion Pond	0	0	0	
Winegar Lake	0	0	0	
Fern Lake	2	0	2	
Tanager Lake	0	0	0	
Subtotal	**22**	**4**	**26**	
Upper Snake River/Targhee National Forest				P: G. Lust; O: S. Patla (9/15)
Ernest Lake	2	0	2	
Bergman Reservoir	0	0	0	Dry; marsh remains wet
Indian Lake	2	3	5	One small cygnet
Squirrel Meadows	4	0	4	2 pairs
Widget Lake	0	0	0	
Junco Lake	0	0	0	
Moose Lake	0	0	0	
Loon Lake	0	0	0	
Rock Lake	0	0	0	
Fish Lake	0	0	0	
Grassy Lake Reservoir	0	0	0	
Subtotal	**8**	**3**	**11**	
Bridger-Teton National Forest-Jackson				
Arizona Lake	0	0	0	
Blackrock Ranger Station pond/sloughs	0	0	0	Site added in 2002
Enos Lake South	0	0	0	
Enos Lake North	2	0	2	
Bridger Lake	0	0	0	
Atlantic Creek	0	0	0	Site not occupied
Lily Lake	2	0	2	Nest failed
Pinto Pond	2	1	3	Cygnet almost fully grown
Tracy Lake	0	0	0	
Burnt Fork Potholes	0	0	0	Water low
Upper Slide Lake	2	0	2	Did not nest
Goose Lake	0	0	0	Completely dry
Grizzly Pond	0	0	0	
Subtotal	**8**	**1**	**9**	
Grand Teton National Park				
Polecat Slough	0	0	0	Site added 2002
Elk Ranch Reservoir	2	0	2	Pair did not nest
Hedrick Pond	0	0	0	One adult died in spring and other left
Swan Lake	2	0	2	Pair did not nest
Christian Pond	0	0	0	Site not occupied
Glade Creek south	2	0	2	
Steamboat Mountain	2	3	5	Site added 2002; lost 1 young
Jackson Lake north	0	0	0	

Jackson Lake south	0	0	0	
Two Ocean Lake	2	2	4	Lost 1 young
Subtotal	**10**	**5**	**15**	
National Elk Refuge				
Southwest Main Marsh	2	1	3	Nested highway pond
Northwest Main Marsh	2	0	2	Did not nest
Southeast Main Marsh	2	2	4	Lost 2 cygnets
Northeast Main Marsh	2	0	2	Winegar Springs; did not nest
Miller Springs	0	0	0	
Pierre Pond east	2	1	3	Cygnet well-developed
Pierre Pond west	0	0	0	
Romney Pond #2	0	0	0	
Nowlin Ponds	0	0	0	
Flat Creek north	0	0	0	
Subtotal	**10**	**4**	**14**	
Jackson Area				
Tucker Pits	0	0	0	
Skyline Pond (Puzzleface Ranch)	0	0	0	Occupied through molt
Boyles Hill area	3	0	3	Pair plus single
Highway 98 winter pen	1	0	1	Site added 2002
South Park Unit, Wyoming Game & Fish Dept.	0	0	0	
Subtotal	**4**	**0**	**4**	
Upper Green River (north of Warren Bridge)				
Mosquito Lake	2	0	2	Did not nest
Wagon Creek Lake	1	0	1	
Rock Crib Lake	0	0	0	
Mud Lake	0	0	0	Pair gone, nest failed, lost 2 young
Roaring Fork Pond	0	0	0	Dry
Dollar Lakes	2	0	2	North lake; patagial tag #8 right wing
Upper Green River above Big Bend	4	0	4	Site added 2002
Green River Big Bend to Black Butte	2	0	2	Site added 2002
Green River Black Butte to Warren Bridge				Site added 2002
Spade Slough	0	0	0	Swan decoy on pond
New Forks Potholes/Marsh Creek	2	0	2	Wild pair, 4 released yearlings in area
Kendal Wetland	0	0	0	
New Fork River (north of highway 191)	0	0	0	1 released yearling with satellite tag
Kitchen Reservoir north	0	0	0	3 yearlings molted here July-August
Kitchen Ranch Reservoir main	2	4	6	Cygnets well-developed
Soda Lakes area	0	0	0	Site added 2002
Subtotal	**15**	**4**	**19**	

Appendix A. (cont.)

New Fork River & Big Sandy to Farson area				
New Fork River Pinedale to Boulder	0	0	0	
Boulder Sloughs	0	0	0	
Oliver (formerly Jenson) Slough	2	0	2	Did not nest
Swift Reservoir	0	0	0	
Big Sandy/Big Bend				Area flown for cranes 9/11; no swans
Big Sandy/Eden reservoirs				Area flown for cranes 9/11; no swans
Farson area				Ponds dry; used in previous years
Subtotal	**2**	**0**	**2**	
Seedskadee NWR (SNWR) and lower Green River				
Main Marsh Hawley, SNWR	0	0	0	Drained for repairs
Main Marsh Hawley 2, SNWR	1	0	1	In small pool; drained for repairs
North Marsh Hamp, SNWR	0	0	0	Drained for repairs
Sagebrush Wetland, SNWR	2	0	2	Site added in 2002
Dunkle Wetland, SNWR	0	0	0	Dry; site added in in 2002
Green River south of Highway 28, SNWR	7	0	7	2 groups - 5 and 2; site added in 2002
Green River Highway 28 to dam, SNWR	1	0	1	East of Hawley Unit; site added in 2002
Fontenelle Reservoir	0	0	0	
Big Piney cutoff, Green River	0	0	0	
Dry Piney Creek area, Green River	0	0	0	
La Barge pond (private)	0	0	0	New oil well near pond; water muddy
McNaughton Reservoir, Hamm's Fork	0	0	0	
Hamm's Fork north of Kemmerer	0	0	0	Site added in 2002
Subtotal	**11**	**0**	**11**	
Salt River				
Palisades Reservoir, Targhee National Forest	1	0	1	
Kibby wetland, Alpine	2	0	2	Nest failed
Salt River, Alpine to Freedom	0	0	0	New location 2002
Salt River, Freedom to Afton	0	0	0	New location 2002
Subtotal	**3**	**0**	**3**	
Other Wyoming				
Swamp Lake, Sunlight Basin	1	0	1	
Colony Site, eastern Wyoming	0	0	0	Not counted in state total; Lacreek birds
Subtotal	**1**	**0**	**1**	
Nevada				O: J. Mackay, M. Collins; P: R. Cassinelli (9/25)
Ruby Lake NWR	24	0	24	
Franklin Lake	0	0	0	Dry

Appendix A. (cont.)

Oregon				
Malheur NWR	14	7	21	M. Laws, R. Roy, T. Hallock, D. Morris, A. Renc, K. Vargas
Summer Lake Wildlife Management Area	2	0	2	M. St. Louis
Lower Chewaucan Marsh				
Upper Chewaucan Marsh				
Paulina Marsh				
Sycan Marsh				
Upper Williamson River				
Klamath Marsh NWR				
Ward/Lily Lakes				
Swan Lake Valley				
Sprague River				
Upper Crooked River				
Thompson Reservoir				
Rivers End Ranch				
Whiskey Creek				

[a]Blank denotes area not surveyed.

Appendix B. Personnel who conducted the 2002 Fall Trumpeter Swan Survey in the U.S.

Montana (Red Rock Lakes NWR, Centennial Valley, Madison Valley)
    Observers: S. Comeau and G. Dehmers (Red Rock Lakes NWR)
    Pilot: B. Twist (Western Montana Aviation)

Montana (Paradise Valley)
    Observer: T. McEneaney (Yellowstone National Park)
    Pilot: R. Stradley (Yellowstone National Park)

Idaho
    Observer: C. Mitchell (Gray's Lake NWR)
    Pilot: G. Lust (Mountain Air Research)

Wyoming
    Observer: S. Patla (Wyoming Game and Fish Department)
    Pilot: G. Lust (Mountain Air Research)

Wyoming (Yellowstone National Park)
    Observer: T. McEneaney (Yellowstone National Park)
    Pilot: R. Stradley (Yellowstone National Park)

Ruby Lake NWR and vicinity
    Observers: J. Mackay and M. Collins (Ruby Lake NWR)
    Pilot: R. Cassinelli (El Aero Services)

Malheur NWR
    M. Laws, R. Roy, T. Hallock, D. Morris, A. Renc, and K. Vargas (Malheur NWR)

Summer Lake WMA
    M. St. Louis (Oregon Department of Fish and Wildlife)